A Work in Progress

A Scriptural Course toward Self-Improvement

CARLA KRAZL

In honor of Annette,
who showed me
what "Bible study" means.
First caller!

—cak—

3558 S. Jefferson Avenue, St. Louis, MO 63118-3968

1-800-325-3040 · www.cph.org

Cover and interior art: iStockphoto.com

Manufactured in the United States of America

1 2 3 4 5 6 7 8 9 10 24 23 22 21 20 19 18 17 16 15

Table of Contents

how to use this book

A ***Work in Progress:*** *A Scriptural Course toward Self-Improvement* is appropriate for any small group, high school age and up. Each of the seven topics covered here is designed to be discussed during a forty-five- to sixty-minute session.

Each Bible study group is unique; therefore this book is intentionally adaptable. Your group may have one dedicated leader, for example, who guides everyone through each session, keeps discussions on track, and leads the group in prayer. An alternative approach is to have group members take turns leading a session (or two). Or perhaps one person guides the group's discussions while another leads everyone in prayer.

You are encouraged to read each session on your own before your study group meets. Take time for personal reflection—your thoughts matter! Working individually, you have an opportunity to think at your own pace, dwelling on the parts that are meaningful to you. This is the time to answer the questions from *your* point of view. At the group study, answers become collaborative. Participants will recognize varying perspectives and hear how others understand the topic. In contemplating the thoughts of others, participants will discover more richness in God's Word.

For each session, you are directed to go to your Bible to read God's Word and then talk about that session's emphasis. Questions are designed to keep group members engaged in personal reflection and in group discussion so the topic is addressed completely. There are a few blanks to fill in along the way. Space is allowed in the margins for noting wisdom gained during group discussions.

There is guidance for life application at the end of each session. Use these opportunities to set small goals for personal betterment—after all, we are all works in progress!

prologue

Teacher.

That is God so frequently!

He taught Pharaoh some lessons, taught the Israelites His commandments, taught Joshua to trust Him, and taught Zechariah that He is in charge.

He taught Nicodemus the necessity of being born again (John 3). He taught the Samaritan woman about living water (John 4) and taught His disciples about the bread of life (John 6). He taught the Pharisees the greatest commandments (Matthew 22) and taught the disciples how to pray (Matthew 6).

Jesus' friends called Him "Teacher." His opponents called Him "Teacher." Those who merely knew *of* Him called Him "Teacher." Certainly, today we think of God as our teacher. But let us be careful not to pigeonhole God; He does more than teach! We can look more closely at other Bible stories and discover more potential titles for God:

1. **Commander.** Noah, in Genesis 6, heard quite a list of directions from God: Build an ark! 450 feet long! Door in the side! And we read in verse 22 that "Noah did this; he did all that God commanded him."
2. **Leader.** The children of Israel, while in the desert after their escape from Egypt, were in serious need of direction. "And the Lord went before them by day in a pillar of cloud to lead them along the way, and by night in a pillar of fire to give them light" (Exodus 13:21).
3. **Provider.** The desert-dwelling Israelites were in serious need of sustenance too. God to the rescue! They received "bread from heaven" every day (Exodus 16:1–30).
4. **Guidance Counselor.** Psalm 73:24 points out that God guides us with His counsel. John 16:13 says "When the Spirit of truth comes, He will guide you into all the truth."
5. **Back-up.** "Likewise the Spirit helps us in our weakness. For we do not know what to pray for as we ought, but the Spirit Himself intercedes for us with groanings too deep for words" (Romans 8:26). The Spirit covers for us, just like a friend who knows us well.
6. **Companion.** Psalm 51:11 says, "Cast me not away from Your presence, and take not Your Holy Spirit from me."

"Teach me to do Your will, for You are my God!"
—a prayer of King David, Psalm 143:10

Teacher, Commander, Leader, Provider, Guidance Counselor, Back-up, Companion: these are all characteristics of our loving God. And He teaches, directs, provides, guides, counsels, defends, and accompanies.

Hmm. It sounds like an all-encompassing descriptive title for God could be Coach! He helps, guides, and shapes us each and every day, all day long. He coaches us through highs and lows, joys and sorrows, and everything in between.

But unlike game day, there is no relaxing after the contest is over, and there is no finish line to coast across. In life, we as Christians cannot fight hard for a while and then relax in the shade. We cannot grow to be perfect, then coast through our remaining days. Life is a relentless series of constant personal adjustments. Each of us, as sinners struggling to model Christ, is always a work in progress.

"You call Me Teacher and Lord, and you are right, for so I am."
—Jesus, when speaking to His disciples, John 13:13

Please, God, reveal Yourself to me today. Through Your Word, inspire me to follow in Your ways. Pour Your will into my heart. Through Your Means of Grace, fill my conscience with the forgiveness that is mine through you. In Jesus' name we pray it all.

Amen!

Session A

A Work in Progress: Responsibility

"With great power comes great responsibility."

Introducing . . .

Toddlers have none, children get some, teens want more, and adults accumulate exponentially increasing amounts. Responsibility increases with age. But what about the almighty God? He is as old as time and has no superior. What is His responsibility? Does He owe anything to anyone? Is He accountable to anyone?

This session will explore answers to these questions. As you explore the topic of responsibility, you will see our God's commitment to His creation. (Is that salvation we see arriving on the horizon?)

The session then details six categories of responsibility that God has unpacked for us in His Word. Responsibility can be shouldered or shirked, accepted or ignored. Here we will hear the directives God gives for His people. These expectations, combined with knowledge that God acts responsibly for us, will lead us to act responsibly for ourselves and for others.

Get Going!

Do you know the source of the quote used for the title of this session: "With great power comes great responsibility"? Think a minute.

When your group meets, find out how many initially thought, "Spider-Man!" The quote is, in fact, directly from the 2002 movie "Spider-Man." Earlier comics often credit Parker's Uncle Ben, who either spoke or implied the sentiment. But Spidey is a quote thief. Nineteenth-century French philosopher Voltaire should also get a nod because he expressed these words when he put pen to paper in his 1832 *Œuvres de Voltaire, volume 48.* Our French buddy, Voltaire, just may have been inspired by Luke 12:48, where the following is found: "Everyone to whom much was given, of him much will be required."

What does it mean to be responsible?

Think about this question in terms of generalities. Add more examples to the following list:

- Take care of duties.
- Answer for actions.
- Endure consequences.
- Be trustworthy.

Next, approach the question from a different angle. List some more possible endings to this sentence: "When I show responsibility, I . . . "

- Plan ahead.
- Have what I need when I need it.
- Meet timelines and deadlines.
- Stay safe.
- Help others do all of these things, too.

What are we responsible for?

We mow the grass we grow, feed the children we birth, carry liability insurance for accidents we cause, and mop up our spills. Society expects people to be responsible for what they have and what they make. And this leads us into:

Society's expectation of God

Can society expect God to be responsible?

He is almighty God, with no superior, so He is responsible *to* no one. But we certainly can talk about what God is responsible *for*. See how He fully accepts the responsibility for the creation that He made:

> Look at the birds of the air: they neither sow nor reap nor gather into barns, and yet your heavenly Father feeds them. Matthew 6:26

> Cast your burden on the Lord, and He will sustain you; He will never permit the righteous to be moved. Psalm 55:22

God provides for our earthly needs of both body and spirit. But wait! There's more!

> Listen to Me, O house of Jacob, all the remnant of the house of Israel, who have been borne by Me from before your birth, carried from the womb; even to your old age I am He, and to gray hairs I will carry you. I have made, and I will bear; I will carry and will save. Isaiah 46:3–4

> Kings shall be your foster fathers, and their queens your nursing mothers. With their faces to the ground they shall bow down to you, and lick the dust of your feet. Then you will know that I am the Lord; those who wait for Me shall not be put to shame. Isaiah 49:23

In these two Isaiah passages, the Lord makes promises to the nation of Israel. He shows His commitment to upholding His responsibility: "I have made, and I will bear; I will carry and will save." Yes, He did make, bear, carry, and save Israel, didn't He? And what about "those who wait for Me"? Were they put to shame? No, those who long waited for the Messiah were able to say, "Here He is! Just as He said! See? My forefathers were not crazy!" He was faithful to Israel, just as He promised. He did what He said He would. And because God has proven Himself faithful to His past promises, we, too, can have confidence in His faithfulness to us.

> Christ loved the church and gave Himself up for her, that He might sanctify her, having cleansed her by the washing of water with the word. Ephesians 5:25–26

"Look at the birds of the air: they neither reap nor gather into barns, and yet your heavenly Father feeds them."
—Matthew 6:26

In this verse, "the church" is defined as all believers in Christ throughout all time and space. In other words, Jesus Christ loved the whole Christian population, past, present, and future. Here we see God's great display of responsibility: God the Father has made something (humanity!) and is taking care of it. He knew Jesus would defeat the devil from the moment that humanity was created. Genesis 3:15 tells us "[God] will put enmity between you and the woman, and between your offspring and her offspring; He shall bruise your head, and you shall bruise His heel." This is the prophecy of Jesus defeating Satan, and *that* is some advance planning! God proved Himself trustworthy—He kept His promise to send the Messiah. And sending the grace of Jesus is the epitome of taking care of what He made.

Yes, God's Word proves that society can expect God to be responsible.

God's expectation of *us*

At the time of creation, God appointed us to be the caretakers of His creation (Genesis 1:16–28). And He calls each of us to be responsible for all aspects of our earthly life. That call is summarized in the following single verse and expounded upon in the six subsequent categories.

> For each will have to bear his own load. Galatians 6:5

The six categories of responsibility

1. Legal

> Exodus 20; The Ten Commandments
>
> Let every person be subject to the governing authorities. For there is no authority except from God, and those that exist have been instituted by God. Romans 13:1
>
> Then [Jesus] said to them, "Therefore render to Caesar the things that are Caesar's, and to God the things that are God's." Matthew 22:21

Refer to the explanation of the Fourth Commandment in the Small Catechism. We have a responsibility to uphold the laws established by God and to respect both natural and instituted authorities. So, what is our response when a governing authority establishes civic law that is contrary to God's Law? That debate always ends with God's Law superseding man's law.

Summarize what God expects our legal responsibilities to be:

2. Moral

> Go to the ant, O sluggard; consider her ways, and be wise. Without having any chief, officer, or ruler, she prepares her bread in summer and gathers her food in harvest. Proverbs 6:6–8

God's directive for us is clear: Plan ahead!

* * * * *

> It is required of stewards that they be found faithful.
> 1 Corinthians 4:2

A trust is something that one hands over to another with the expectation that it will be well cared for. It is as if one says, "Here. This is mine, but I would like for you to have it for a while; please take good care of it." That is exactly what God does when He gives each of us physical blessings. "Our" children are really *His* children, whom He asks us to care for and love. Our country is His country that we need to respect. Our yard is His creation for which we are responsible. When the Bible study group gathers, work together to see how many "entrusted items" you can list. Count them as you go!

* * * * *

> To one he gave five talents, to another two, to another one, to each according to his ability. Matthew 25:15

This verse is the summary of the parable found in Matthew 25:14–30. In Jesus' story, the master was going on a journey and entrusted his three servants with money. A *lot* of money. When he returned, the master held each accountable for the wise use of his money. Jesus makes a point through this parable, showing that we all are accountable for using our blessings responsibly! After all . . .

Whom do our "talents" (money or skills) benefit?

To whom or for whom must we show moral responsibility?

3. Family

Family members are part of our legal and moral responsibility, but now we focus on family as a responsibility category of its own. These verses will zero in on God's directive to treat our family with respect and honor.

> Honor your father and your mother. Exodus 20:12

This is a popular verse for parents of toddlers and teens!

What does* honor *mean?

Write your thoughts below to help guide your thoughts later during the group discussion:

***Do you consider* respect *to be a synonym for* honor?**

Take some time to compare and contrast *honor* with *respect*. List similarities and differences between the two concepts.

The words are similar in that they both indicate holding someone in high regard. Yet the words are different in that *respect* acknowledges someone's position, while *honor* acknowledges their worth. This subtle difference makes it easy for us to see far beyond simply obeying mom and dad. We are responsible for treating them as the God-established assets they are. They receive their greatest worth from the fact that God established them.

* * * * *

> And these words that I command you today shall be on your heart. You shall teach them diligently to your children, and shall talk of them when you sit in your house, and when you walk by the way, and when you lie down, and when you rise. Deuteronomy 6:6–7

> Train up a child in the way he should go; even when he is old he will not depart from it. Proverbs 22:6

In addition to the responsibility of feeding their children, God has charged parents with teaching their kids how to be faithful and responsible adults! That is some heavy stuff and perhaps the weightiest task felt by parents.

* * * * *

> Let each one of you love his wife as himself, and let the wife see that she respects her husband. Ephesians 5:33

Proverbs 22 may tell of parents' weightiest task, but Ephesians 5 summarizes one of the most *challenging* tasks for some married people. To show this love and respect at all times can be difficult. Yet, clearly, it IS God's expectation of us.

4. Community

> Remind them to be submissive to rulers and authorities, to be obedient, to be ready for every good work. Titus 3:1

Initially, being "submissive to rulers and authorities" sounds restrictive. After all, our rulers have a list of things we cannot do. But then again, there is this document called the Constitution of the United States. In it, the rulers and authorities clearly delineate a list of things that we, as citizens, *can* do: worship our chosen deity, speak our mind, assemble at will, bear arms. Gerald W. Johnson, a noted journalist and historian (1890–1980), once remarked on how the gift of a right also saddles a man with responsibility. A right to free speech does, technically, give you a pass to speak harshly, speak critically, and speak, as some might say, "without a filter." But what Mr. Johnson points out is that speakers have a duty to act with the interest of the community in mind. Speak to build up, not to tear down. Use freedoms wisely. God says it this way:

> For each will have to bear his own load. Galatians 6:5

"For we are His workmanship, created in Christ Jesus for good works, which God prepared beforehand, that we should walk in them."
—Ephesians 2:10

> But exhort one another every day, as long as it is called "today," that none of you may be hardened by the deceitfulness of sin. Hebrews 3:13

God calls us to encourage everyone not just in our own home or with our own friends but also in the community at large. We have a responsibility for ensuring that our public actions, overheard discussions, and social media posts are all edifying to the society in which we live.

In summary, our community responsibility includes wise use of our what?

answer on page 85

5. Faith

Matthew 25:1–13

While studying on your own, grab your Bible and read the parable. It is the parable of the ten virgins, each girl being responsible for her own lamp while awaiting the bridegroom's arrival. Be careful! You might miss the show if you aren't prepared! Likewise, each of us has a responsibility to guard our heart's faith. The alternative is to be caught with an empty heart and not be prepared for Jesus' second coming on Judgment Day.

* * * * *

Acts 18:1–6

In these verses, Paul is preaching Christ as Messiah and the listening Jews get abusive. Paul, obviously frustrated, says he is *done* with these people: "I have fulfilled my responsibility!" What does this story indicate that *our* responsibility is? It is each Christian's responsibility to witness to Jesus' work and promise of salvation, to testify that Jesus is the Christ.

We are responsible for guarding ________________ faith and the faith of ________________.

answer on page 85

6. Personal

> Everyone to whom much was given, of him much will be required, and from him to whom they entrusted much, they will demand the more. Luke 12:48

You are the only one who can fulfill your potential. And did you notice? This is not a request. Fulfill your potential!

* * * * *

> For we are His workmanship, created in Christ Jesus for good works, which God prepared beforehand, that we should walk in them. Ephesians 2:10

God is our Creator. He is the one who gives us our potential. He knows what we are capable of and has prepared the way for us to be able to fulfill it!

Make note of one way that you will, today, fulfill the potential God gave you. Make note of one way that you will decide what type of person you will be today. It may be the same answer!

> Therefore, my beloved brothers, be steadfast, immovable, always abounding in the work of the Lord, knowing that in the Lord your labor is not in vain. 1 Corinthians 15:58

Often, our work is satisfying and we feel good about it. But other times, our work time feels like wasted time, wasted effort; there is not a big enough payoff for anyone. In those times, how can we know that our labor is not in vain? We know because all of our work is labor in the Lord. Our work is to fulfill responsibilities big and small to ourselves, our families, and our neighbors. Even if we see little payoff, our work is not in vain, for it gives glory to God. Our work then attests to our joy in God's promise of our salvation.

You may have heard people push the notion of works righteousness, that is, the idea that we do good things in order to earn God's favor. One might interpret 1 Corinthians 15:58 that way. It could be read from the perspective that our "work of the Lord" will earn us "points" with God. Alas, that is far from the truth! Jesus works redemption based on faith alone, not on works (Romans 8:1). His mercy and grace come to us through His Word, through the Lord's Supper, and through Baptism. God does not need our good works.

In addition to grace, God has also given us a free will. It is God who chooses us, brings us to faith—not the other way around. But outside of spiritual matters, we are free to choose our actions. The beauty of God's system is that we are not required to do good for our own benefit, but we freely choose to serve God and others *because* of His love for us. Our actions are a byproduct of our faith.

Work in Progress: Taking It Home

During your group study session, wrap up by giving one another a chance to say any final comments or ask final questions. Review the categories of responsibility spoken of in this session: legal, moral, family, community, faith, and personal responsibilities. Discuss the following questions.

Which category do you feel you could give more attention to?

How will you try to increase your show of responsibility this coming week or month?

Now encourage one another to share goals with the rest of your group. Sharing answers aloud adds a bit of accountability and gives people the courage to follow through on their thoughts!

Before closing with prayer, be reminded of God's loving grace—that we do not have to be perfect, for He freely forgives us for not upholding our responsibilities. God took on responsibility by creating us: He has promised to care for us, His people, and He sent His Son, Jesus, to hand us all salvation!

Have the group leader or a volunteer close the session with prayer. Include prayer requests from group participants, or say the following prayer together:

Heavenly Father, it is so easy to get weighed down and feel burdened by the list of responsibilities we have. There are so many! Help us to be wise in evaluating our duties. Help us each to manage our list according to Your will. Let each of us know that You have fulfilled Your responsibility to us in sending Jesus to be our Savior. And help us to feel the warmth of Your providence as You continue to fulfill Your responsibility of carrying us. It is in Jesus' name that we pray.

And all God's people say,

Amen!

Session B

A Work in Progress: Respect

Raise your hand if you agree with Aretha!

Introducing . . .

The previous session touched on the definition of respect. In this session, we will get out a magnifying glass and pick apart the concept and practice of respect. Each member of your group will explore her own thoughts on the matter and then hear the numerous ways that God's Word addresses the all-important attitude.

The second part of this session delves into the idea of respecting a name. Not just the letters, not just the word—the group will discover what respecting a name really entails and will come away knowing the awesome power of God.

Get going!

To set the tone, have someone play some Aretha Franklin music at the beginning of your group meeting. Make sure the playlist concludes with "Respect."

Just what does it mean to be respectful?

Don't rush to answer this question. Allow plenty of time for thoughts to percolate and responses to come. Think of a few examples. When your group gathers, each member of the group can contribute to a collective definition.

answer on page 86

What and whom are we to respect?

Take some time with this question as well. Challenge your group to come up with a list of twenty responses—or fifty! Are there even more?

Of all the people and things we respect, God, in His Word, provides us with an all-inclusive list of what and who we *must* respect. These verses give us some clues:

> Then God said, "Let us make man in Our image, after Our likeness. And let them have dominion over the fish of the sea and over the birds of the heavens and over the livestock and over all the earth and over every creeping thing that creeps on the earth." Genesis 1:26
>
> Honor everyone. Love the brotherhood. Fear God. 1 Peter 2:17
>
> And Jesus said, "You shall not murder, You shall not commit adultery, You shall not steal, You shall not bear false witness, Honor your father and mother, and, You shall love your neighbor as yourself." Matthew 19:18–19

God's Word summarizes three categories of what and whom we are to respect in our world. They are:

The environment **Others** **Self**

Everything we should respect falls into these categories. Well, except for that one other entity . . .

* * * * *

What kind of respect does God expect?

"You shall have no other gods before Me." Exodus 20:3

If there were a list of "Things to Respect," God and His First Commandment would be at the top of it. Does that mean the First Commandment is God's most important rule? The numerical ranking does not make it the most important, but the *content* does. First and foremost, in everything in life, we are commanded to hold God in the highest place of ultimate respect.

> It is the Lord your God you shall fear. Him you shall serve and by His name you shall swear. Deuteronomy 6:13

> Let all the earth fear the Lord; let all the inhabitants of the world stand in awe of Him! Psalm 33:8

These two verses are directive, like the First Commandment, and they get specific. These verses are examples of God's Law. God's Law is the collective group of His expectations for us: what He says we must or must not do.

How would you define fear?

Put your hand over the next paragraph and think for yourself before reading on!

Fear is commonly described as a feeling or emotion brought on by anticipated pain. But this discussion is not about being scared. This is a Bible study, after all; someone will pull out the Sunday School answer that "fear is a healthy, God-size respect." *Merriam-Webster's Collegiate Dictionary* says that *to fear* is "to have a reverential awe of." *Awe* is a word that tells of speechless admiration of a magnificent power. Awe implies a child-like wonder for a brilliant presence. When awe is combined with reverence, it is the kind of fear that God demands of us.

> Blessed is the man who fears the Lord, who greatly delights in His commandments! Psalm 112:1

Here we begin to see verses that have a promise connected to the directive. Another example of this is the Fourth Commandment, which demands respect (Honor your father and mother) and comes with a promise ("that your days may be long in the land that the LORD your God is giving you," Exodus 20:12).

> The fear of the LORD leads to life, and whoever has it rests satisfied; he will not be visited by harm. Proverbs 19:23

Is there anyone in the world who is never visited by harm? (And the crowd choruses a sarcastic, "Yeah, right!") Our world is full of troubles, everything from personal struggles to natural disasters. This worldwide imperfection is a result of man's fall into sin (Genesis 3). But still, understanding that God allows these troubles to happen is hard to swallow. Here's the thing: Part of fearing the Lord is knowing that He has the power to handle our troubles for us. Part of fearing the Lord is trusting that God is bigger than any earthly struggle or calamity. Fear is knowing that we can rest in God's promise of salvation.

> And He will be the stability of your times, abundance of salvation, wisdom, and knowledge; the fear of the LORD is Zion's treasure. Isaiah 33:6

The awe we have for the Lord is what gives us our sure foundation.

Back around to how God wants us to show respect to others

> [Jesus said,] "You shall love the Lord your God with all your heart and with all your soul and with all your strength and with all your mind, and your neighbor as yourself." Luke 10:27

This is one of the eight times the Bible uses the phrase "Love your neighbor as yourself." *Eight times!* Keep in mind that our neighbor is any other person with whom we share space or time. And certainly, part of loving that neighbor is showing him respect.

Unscramble the letters to discover things we should respect in every individual:

N I L E S E G F

P O I N N S O I

I H R S T G

E U A S L V

answer on page 86

Respecting these things in others makes it possible for humanity to work together, live together, and grow together. Following is a quote from an unknown, but astute, pen:

"We need to respect others to collaborate; we need to collaborate to live."

Just what does that mean?

Take some time to think about it. Write your thoughts here, then be prepared to talk about it with your group.

Collaborations are often challenging because no one is really in charge, no one person is the expert, everyone has different ideas, and sometimes no one really knows what to prioritize. Involved parties brainstorm, suggest, compromise, and theorize. Only through equalized respect and willingness to listen and consider is revelation discovered and progress made. Society advances through this cooperative work style of recognition, deference, and establishment.

* * * * *

List a few people you respect:

These folks may include may include historical figures, parents, people much older than you, acquaintances, children, and people from your high school days, et cetera.

Considering each person you listed, did you know this person and grow to respect him or her, or did you respect before getting to know him or her?

If you respected this person while you simply "knew of" him or her, that means you respected his or her name. Read on to expand on this idea of "respecting a name."

Names identify us in all the spheres of our lives: in our family, workplace, legal dealings. Nicknames further identify us. A person may acquire a nickname for a variety of reasons. Perhaps he shares his given name with others. Maybe his father is also named Tim or there are three Michaels in the class. Our name reflects who we are; it brings up associations in the minds of those who simply know *of* us. We all want good and honorable things and feelings associated with our names. That is why the phrase "make a name for yourself" exists.

Used in this way, a person's name can indicate a good reputation or a questionable one. A good name can be a powerful force for opening doors and making things happen.

* * * * *

What does God say about names?

> You shall not take the name of the LORD your God in vain.
> Exodus 20:7

Another commandment, this time the second.

What do you understand* in vain *to mean?

Merriam-Webster's Collegiate Dictionary defines *in vain* as "in an irreverent or blasphemous manner." Using God's name, *any* of His names, with an empty, useless, or false intent is wrong. And to quote God, "you shall not." Again, no suggestions.

* * * * *

> [A whole bunch of leaders] said, "Stand up and bless the LORD your God from everlasting to everlasting. Blessed be Your glorious name, which is exalted above all blessing and praise." Nehemiah 9:5

> I will extol You, my God and King, and bless Your name forever and ever. Every day I will bless You and praise Your name forever and ever. Psalm 145:1–2

"I will extol You, my God and King, and bless Your name forever and ever. Every day I will bless You and praise Your name forever and ever."
—Psalm 145:1–2

David does an abundance of "name praising" in the Psalms. What exactly is the big deal about God's NAME? Read on!

The story of Peter healing the crippled beggar at the temple gate is found in Acts, beginning with verse 3:1. Read the whole event in the Bible on your own. In your group study, share the following summation and selected verses.

A beggar sat at the temple gate every day. Peter and John walked by, and the beggar asked them for money, as he did everyone else who passed by. And then . . .

> Peter said, "I have no silver and gold, but what I do have I give to you. In the name of Jesus Christ of Nazareth, rise up and walk!" Acts 3:6

So this guy got up and was dancing all over! Can you imagine? While he was kind of making a fool of himself, a crowd began to gather. They were asking who Peter and John were and were saying things like, "Wow! That man has never walked a step in his whole life. These must be great men to do this!" Peter and John replied, "Why does this surprise you? Why do you stare as if it were us? Jesus, the one you crucified, did this."

> And [Jesus'] name—by faith in His name—has made this man strong whom you see and know, and the faith that is through Jesus has given the man this perfect health in the presence of you all. Acts 3:16

With the crowd gathered, Peter and John stepped through the door that the miracle had opened and preached the Gospel: "Repent and be forgiven! The Christ has come!" Now the Jewish priests and Sadducees were not happy about this Christianity stuff. That night, Peter and John were thrown in the slammer. The next day, they were questioned: "By what power or what name did you do this?" Peter replied:

> [It is] by the name of Jesus Christ of Nazareth. . . . There is salvation in no one else, for there is no other name under heaven given among men by which we must be saved. Acts 4:10, 12

Peter's statement really got under the chief priest's skin. But lacking a real crime of which to convict them, the priest just commanded them not to speak in the name of Jesus anymore. Their reply? "Whether it is right in the sight of God to listen to you rather than to God, you must judge, for we cannot but speak of what we have seen and heard" (Acts 4:19–20). And then:

> When [the council] had further threatened them, they let them go, finding no way to punish them, because of the people, for all were praising God for what had happened. Acts 4:21

Look at that witness! Go back over the previous five Bible references in Acts and mark the instances where the name of Jesus is mentioned or referred to. Look at the power of that name! No wonder God expects us to respect it.

The name of Jesus has been given to us too. After discussing the power of His name, perhaps your group can beef up the value ascribed to the name "Christian." This name was given to us at our Baptism and truly marks us as the Redeemed of Christ. Christ has died on the cross for us, done the work of redemption for us, and then completely gifted it to us. Ahhhh! Don't you *love* that name?!

Work in Progress: Taking It Home

What did you learn, realize, or connect during this session that was new to you? Maybe something quickly comes to mind, or maybe you have to look back over the study pages for a reminder.

Share your revelations with the rest of the members in your group, no matter how minor, if you are willing. A group discussion almost always leads to new insights! And new insights can lead to new possibilities.

How can you use this new insight to better yourself this coming week or month?

As a group, wrap up your discussion. Either your group leader or a volunteer should close the session with a prayer. Include prayer requests from group participants, or say the following prayer together:

Our dear God, today our hearts are full of respect for You because of the way in which You impart Your grace—completely, certainly, and without any merit on our part. Our heads are full of respect for You because of the ways You care for us and provide for all of our needs.

Please, Lord, help us, for we are weak. Forgive us for times we disrespect You and show callousness toward You and toward others. Make us each a blessing to our neighbor. Give to all of us both the opportunity and the guts to boldly proclaim the power of Your name! It is in Jesus' name we pray.

And all God's people say,

Amen!

Session C

A Work in Progress: Compassion

Are you in the "Me" generation?

Introducing . . .

"I feel for you."

"I wish it were me, not you."

"What can I do to help?"

Compassion is a natural human emotion and often a response that seems involuntary. We feel hurt on behalf of another. We want to comfort the baby who cries, dust off the child who falls, boost the classmate or co-worker who struggles. But do we always get it right? Is our compassion perfect? Nope. Sometimes our human compassion is driven by thankfulness that "it didn't happen to me." Sometimes we help because others are watching. Sometimes we want to bank a good deed so we can get help when we need it. (There's that selfishness alarm going off again!)

To set our feelings of compassion on the right track, this session opens with examples of how God shows compassion to His people. Through these verses, participants will see the reality of our need for a compassionate God. Through discussion of the parable of the Good Samaritan, we will see the link between needing compassion and giving compassion. Sinners have the ability and mindset to show compassion when they know and feel the compassion that our loving God gives. Faithful Christians are now ready to hear God's directive to be compassionate and forgiving to others.

Get going!

As the members of your group settle in, begin with a discussion of the names of generations. See how many other generations the group can list. (Write them in the space at the top of the next page.) Think "Baby Boomers," et cetera. Can you put them in order?

Talk about the differences in generations. The *me generation* was a term coined along the way that indicated the selfish direction in which society seemed to be headed. Today's discussion about compassion is quite the opposite of that looking-out-for-number-one attitude.

What does it mean to be compassionate? Think about a definition, and think of some varying examples.

answer on page 87

Why do you show compassion?

This may be a sensitive, personal question for you or for others in your group. Possible answers could include: because of love, obligation, or even guilt.

Let's start with God

God showed compassion toward His people:

> But the LORD was gracious to them and had compassion on them, and He turned toward them, because of His covenant with Abraham, Isaac, and Jacob. 2 Kings 13:23

This was after King Hazael, just one in a long list of tyrannical kings, oppressed Israel. God said He would look out for Israel, and He did. Read on—

> You in Your great mercies did not forsake them in the wilderness. The pillar of cloud to lead them in the way did not depart from them by day, nor the pillar of fire by night to light for them the way by which they should go. You gave Your good Spirit to instruct them and did not withhold Your manna. Nehemiah 9:19–20

Verses 19 and 20 are an excerpt from a description of a festival in which the Israelites were praising God and thanking Him for His providence through the years. These verses point out the compassion God showed to the wandering Israelites even after they had made the golden calf and called it their god. That compassion, that care! Then the Israelites were happy for a long time. They survived their time in the desert, then had kingdoms and nations and reveled "in [God's] great goodness. Nevertheless, they were disobedient and rebelled against [God] and cast [God's] law behind their back" (Nehemiah 9:25–26). And God became unhappy:

> Therefore [God] gave [Israel] into the hand of their enemies, who made them suffer. And in the time of their suffering they cried out to You and You heard them from heaven, and according to Your great mercies You gave them saviors who saved them from the hand of their enemies. Nehemiah 9:27

Aren't we often like that in our personal lives? We're happy and content, feeling faithful; then we slip into "self-reliant mode," forgetting to place our dependence on God. Life gets tough, and it's then that we turn back to God. Over and over that cycle goes. And sure enough, God continues to love and guide, support and forgive us. Our God is a God of compassion! Isaiah says it straightforwardly:

> "In overflowing anger for a moment I hid My face from you, but with everlasting love I will have compassion on you," says the Lord, your Redeemer. Isaiah 54:8

In return, God asks only for our faithfulness.

If your study group is made up of parents, perhaps they can talk about this feeling of "overflowing anger" and hiding for a moment or two. In today's language, that means "taking a deep breath and counting to ten" or "putting yourself in time out." This similarity may give us a little understanding of how God feels about us, His children. Hear this parent/God comparison again in the Psalms:

> As a father shows compassion to his children, so the LORD shows compassion to those who fear Him. Psalm 103:13

Sometimes parents become quite angry with their children, but parents usually find compassion. God always has compassion for us too. And again, our response to God is our belief in the saving work of Jesus Christ. That saving work—Christ bearing death on the cross as payment for our sins, then rising again in defeat of Satan—is the ultimate act of compassion. Thanks, God!

* * * * *

Switching gears just a bit . . .

How many people do you think Jesus healed?

Let's just say a lot. Many of Jesus' healings are related to the ninety-plus references to compassion in the Bible.

Why do you think Jesus healed people?

answer on page 87

Jesus often healed simply because of His compassion:

> And Jesus went throughout all the cities and villages, teaching in their synagogues and proclaiming the gospel of the kingdom and healing every disease and every affliction. When He saw the crowds, He had compassion for them, because they were harassed and helpless, like sheep without a shepherd. Matthew 9:35–36

> When He went ashore He saw a great crowd, and He had compassion on them and healed their sick. Matthew 14:14
>
> Then Jesus called His disciples to Him and said, "I have compassion on the crowd because they have been with Me now three days and have nothing to eat. And I am unwilling to send them away hungry, lest they faint on the way." Matthew 15:32

"When He went ashore He saw a great crowd, and He had compassion on them and healed their sick."
—Matthew 14:14

All of these examples simply say that Jesus loves humankind!

Jesus also teaches about compassion

Read the parable of the Good Samaritan, found in Luke 10:25–37.

Describe the lawyer. Why did he want to "justify himself" (v. 29)?

answer on page 87

How might we explain the lack of compassion from the religious professionals (the priest and the Levite)?

Ponder how you think you would have responded under the same circumstances.

Which brings us to another question: Why do we sometimes have less compassion than we should?

"But God showed His love for us in that while we were still sinners, Christ died for us."
—Romans 5:8

Why do you think Jesus made the hero of the story a Samaritan?

Think and write before you read on!

The Samaritan race was despised by those of Jewish decent. This story of the snubbed saving the snubber is an irony, quite the opposite of what we'd expect. Hmmm. Does that theme sound familiar? We are again reminded of being saved by Someone who has no logical reason to save us. Samaritan saves Jew; Jesus saves me. Why does God show us this compassion? Who knows! He created us and He loves us and that is what He decided to do. *That* is where our faith comes in. God is not required to show compassion. He has no obligation to save us. In fact, because of sin, we are God's enemies. Yet through His mercy, because of His compassion, God has forgiven us. He has saved us through Jesus.

Where do you think the Samaritan might have found his compassion?

Perhaps it was his response to the unpleasantness he had endured because of his own nationality. Or maybe he was just a nice guy. Again, it doesn't matter. Think about where we find our compassion. What is the source?

> But God shows His love for us in that while we were still sinners, Christ died for us. Romans 5:8

The source of our compassion is God; it is our response to the love that God shows to us. We strive to be compassionate through the power of the Holy Spirit. When we show compassion, we are an extension of God's love for us through Jesus.

* * * * *

Here is God's directive to us for showing compassion:

> Finally, all of you, have unity of mind, sympathy, brotherly love, a tender heart, and a humble mind. 1 Peter 3:8
>
> Bear one another's burdens, and so fulfill the law of Christ. Galatians 6:2
>
> Be kind to one another, tenderhearted, forgiving one another, as God in Christ forgave you. Ephesians 4:32
>
> Put on then, as God's chosen ones, holy and beloved, compassionate hearts, kindness, humility, meekness, and patience, bearing with one another and, if one has a complaint against another, forgiving each other; as the Lord has forgiven you, so you also must forgive. Colossians 3:12–13

These verses are God's instructions for our behavior toward others. The words are to the point and the message is clear. Our actions toward others should be compassionate and forgiving, just as our merciful God is compassionate and forgiving toward us. Do our neighbors always deserve our compassion? Do they always earn it? Nope. But still God wants us to give it to them. Do we deserve God's compassion? Have we earned it? Nope. But He gives it to us because of His loving patience. He forgives our sins again and again and again. Amazing grace!

Work in Progress: Taking It Home

What can you do in the coming week or month to show more compassion?

Oh, boy. That's a wide-open question. Write something specific; note a specific part of the day, a certain reoccurring instance, one challenging bit of a co-worker's personality. Small places are good places to start!

Share your answers during the group study. Discuss the challenges of showing compassion in new areas, and predict the benefits of reaching to show more compassion.

Before the session ends, make sure that everyone has a chance to ask any questions or make final comments. End your session with a prayer. Consider a "circle prayer." The leader begins, then each member of the group takes a turn, if desired, to add a petition until the prayer has come full circle back to the leader, who concludes. You may also read the following prayer together:

Dear God, we thank You today for the opportunity to gather together to hear Your words for us from the Word. Life here on earth is a struggle as we fight against our selfish, sinful tendencies. Be with each of us in thought and action. Guide our hearts to recognize the compassion and forgiveness that You show us every day. Let that knowledge build us up. Holy Spirit, guide our minds and hearts to respond by showing others compassion and forgiveness. Help us each to look for and make use of the opportunities you give us to practice and show our neighbors patience and compassion.

Thank You for the greatest gift of compassion: Your Son, Jesus Christ. Thank You for the salvation that is ours to anticipate because of His work. It is in His name we pray. And all God's people say,

Amen!

Session D

A Work in Progress: Peace

One of Frank Costanza's memorable lines

Introducing . . .

Peace is one of those crazy things that everyone wants, dreams of, and runs after, but never holds. Some may touch its shirttail or even grasp a handful for a while, but nobody ever claims it. At least, as a wise man once said, "Not on this side." That is the world we live in, you see, for the wise man was referring to this side of heaven.

Somehow that did not stop God from promoting the topic wholeheartedly in His Word. The Bible addresses no fewer than seven types of peace. This session offers participants the opportunity to take a closer look at these subcategories of peace. We will begin by hearing about the peace that God asks of us. (Of course He has such expectations!) Then the discussion segues into the kinds of peace that God offers us, His gifts to us through His grace, with no deserving or earning on our part at all.

Get going!

Go back and read this session's title. Can your group come up with Frank Costanza's memorable line? It is safe to assume the theme has to do with peace! Costanza was a character on the wildly popular NBC comedy series *Seinfeld*. Still televised today in syndication, the original episodes ran for nine seasons from 1989 to 1998. In one particular episode, short-tempered Frank decided to start a business in his garage with two quarrelsome employees and a meddling wife. He was convinced he could make it all work because of his new, two-word mantra.

answer on page 88

***Brainstorm some terms, phrases, and slang that use the word* peace.**

Take the study group challenge: Who can come up with the longest list? Then see the list of suggestions on page 88.

Peace is the presence of ____________________ and the absence of ____________________.

Take a few minutes to add a handful of words to each blank, and then when your group meets, let each member share thoughts, if she wishes. In doing this, the group will reach a thorough and well-rounded understanding of peace.

answer on page 88

Six types of peace in the Bible

(This session skips over a seventh type of peace—peace as the opposite of war. A half-million times, give or take, the Bible talks of the peace that God brings to the Israelites during all of their Old Testament unrest and warring with other nations. While this peace is a great blessing of God for the Israelites, today's study will focus on peace as it pertains to individuals.)

1. Peaceful relationships

There are oh-so-many Bible references that detail God's instruction for humanity: be peacemakers and lead peaceful lives.

> Deceit is in the heart of those who devise evil, but those who plan peace have joy. Proverbs 12:20
>
> Mark the blameless and behold the upright, for there is a future for the man of peace. But transgressors shall be altogether destroyed; the future of the wicked shall be cut off. Psalm 37:37–38
>
> Turn away from evil and do good; seek peace and pursue it. Psalm 34:14

> Blessed are the peacemakers, for they shall be called sons of God. Matthew 5:9
>
> And a harvest of righteousness is sown in peace by those who make peace. James 3:18

"And a harvest of righteousness is sown in peace by those who make peace." —James 3:18

Clearly, God's message is that we are to "plan peace," be a "man of peace," "seek peace," and make peace. Right now, though, some in the group are thinking, "Great. God wants me to make peace. Wish He were a little more specific about how I can do that. I mean, have you *seen* the people I deal with every day?!"

God's pure, unadulterated peace existed in His creation, the world, right up until the point of sin—the moment that Eve doubted God's statement that man would die after eating from the tree. What destroyed the world's peace? Sin.

Review the previous five Scripture passages. According to God's Word, what is the opposite of peace? Go ahead. Read them again. You have to read between the lines a bit.

The opposite of peace is sin. So . . . God's "how to" is there after all: be a peacemaker by living free from sin. It is a tall order, and He never said it would be easy. But being a peacemaker is definitely another part of His command to love our neighbors.

* * * * *

> Let the peace of Christ rule in your hearts, to which indeed you were called in one body. Colossians 3:15

Jesus had previously used the analogy that Christians are all members of one body, the Church. All members are important, and we all work together. What happens when a person's body is not at peace with itself, when lungs are congested, or there is a pulled hamstring, or the stomach is unsettled? The system is broken and productivity drops or even stops. The body needs a peaceful harmony to run efficiently and effectively. The Church—and the world—needs that peaceful harmony too.

The categories of peace for the remainder of the session focus on God's actions toward us: the peacefulness that God brings His people.

2. Peaceful rest

What is the difference between peace and rest? Peace is always restful. But rest is not always peaceful, especially during times of stress. Most people will agree that rest in the form of a night's sleep comes more quickly and lasts much longer when the day-to-day of life is peaceful.

> Come to Me, all who labor and are heavy laden, and I will give you rest. Take My yoke upon you, and learn from Me, for I am gentle and lowly in heart, and you will find rest for your souls. Matthew 11:28–29

That first sentence, verse 28, sounds easy and perfect—we just ask and God takes away the burden. But then, hold on a minute. "Take My *yoke*?" That sounds more like God is giving us *more* work!

Well, it is work, but we have to look at it through farmer-colored glasses. A yoke links two working animals together; it is one harness around two necks. Often, a farmer would join a calm, experienced animal (we will call him Hank) with a young, undisciplined animal (known here as Junior). Hank knows the farmer's commands and works without distraction. Junior would really like to do his own thing, but that yoke literally makes him a captive audience to Hank's example. He quickly learns the ins and outs of plowing effectively. Matthew 11:29 may be Jesus' shortest parable. The farmer represents God; He is the boss, knows the best way to do stuff, and has the plan. Hank represents Jesus; He follows God's plan and provides a perfect example for Junior to learn from. Junior represents all of humanity. When we try to work alone, the work cannot get done. We cannot get it right. But because the Holy Spirit yokes us to Jesus, we follow His lead under the watchful eye of God. And that is where the rest comes in—it is mental rest, as we do not have to figure it all out on our own.

And then, additionally, there is the "I-can't-possibly-be-carrying-my-share" phenomenon. Now, Hank and Junior represent us. Hank tries to pull something and cannot budge it. He finds Junior to help. Both pull together, and the object moves. After the job is done, they compare notes. They realize that neither one felt like he was bearing his share of the weight. In using the yoke reference, Jesus also knew that working together makes things easier.

3. Peaceful security/safety

> May the Lord give strength to His people! May the Lord bless His people with peace! Psalm 29:11

> But the Lord said to him, "Peace be to you. Do not fear; you shall not die." Then Gideon built an altar there to the Lord and called it, The Lord Is Peace. Judges 6:23–24

Judges 6 tells the story of how Gideon was called by God to save the Israelites from the oppressive Midianites. But even in this story of war, the focus on peace is not simply "the end of war." Gideon was threshing wheat when an angel showed up and said, "The Lord is with you, mighty warrior." Gideon said, "What? Who are you talking about? I'm the weakest of the weak!" The Lord assured Gideon that He would be with him and Israel would defeat the Midianites. Gideon was still not so sure of all of this, so he asked God for a sign and to "please wait while I go prepare a sacrifice." The Lord waited until Gideon brought the meat, bread, and broth sacrifice. The angel touched the sacrifice with the tip of his staff and the whole thing burst into flames. How's *that* for a sign?! Reread the ending of the story; Judges 6:23–24, printed above.

God drops a big change in Gideon's life, plus sets a nice fire and says, "Hey, peace to you, Gideon. Relax. No need to fear." Gideon knew and felt that the Lord was his security.

* * * * *

> As they were talking about these things, Jesus Himself stood among them, and said to them, "Peace to you!" Luke 24:36

This event happened when Jesus appeared to His apostles after His resurrection. When you think about what these men had been through during the previous few days, there is no doubt that the men were a little nervous. Jesus uses the word *peace* in the same context that God did with Gideon. *Peace* again means, "Relax! No need to fear. I am with you, and I have it all under control."

4. A peaceful heart

A peaceful heart is the peace that God affords us through the Holy Spirit. The next passage is Jesus speaking to the disciples after His resurrection. He knows that in dealing with His death and resurrection, the disciples have sustained a major blow. He knows, too, that His impending ascension will be another hit to the fragile guys, and He has this message to share:

> These things I have spoken to you while I am still with you. But the Helper, the Holy Spirit, whom the Father will send in My name, He will teach you all things and bring to your remembrance all that

> I have said to you. Peace I leave with you; My peace I give to you. Not as the world gives do I give to you. Let not your hearts be troubled, neither let them be afraid. John 14:25–27

* * * * *

What does a counselor do for people these days? A counselor listens, guides, reassures, calms, points in the right direction, and pats on the back. That sounds just like the work of our Counselor, the Holy Spirit; He reassures us through the gift of faith.

> Nevertheless, I tell you the truth: it is to your advantage that I go away, for if I do not go away, the Helper will not come to you. But if I go, I will send Him to you. John 16:7

> But when the Helper comes, whom I will send to you from the Father, the Spirit of truth, who proceeds from the Father, He will bear witness about Me. John 15:26

God has promised the presence of His Counselor (Helper).

* * * * *

> And take the helmet of salvation, and the sword of the Spirit, which is the word of God. Ephesians 6:17

> Let not your hearts be troubled, neither let them be afraid. John 14:27

God protects us. God gives us the equipment we need. Through God the Son, we are preserved for eternity. And God the Holy Spirit assures us of that. Now *that* is peace for hearts.

5. Peaceful reconciliation

Read about peace between God and man in the Scripture passage below:

> Therefore remember that at one time you Gentiles in the flesh, called "the uncircumcision" by what is called the circumcision, which is made in the flesh by hands—remember that you were at that time separated from Christ, alienated from the commonwealth of Israel and strangers to the covenants of promise, having no hope and without God in the world. But now in Christ Jesus you who once were far off have been brought near by the blood of Christ. For He Himself is our peace, who has made us both one and has broken down in His flesh the dividing wall of hostility by abolishing the law of commandments expressed in ordinances, that He might create in Himself one new man in place of the two,

> so making peace, and might reconcile us both to God in one body through the cross, thereby killing the hostility. And He came and preached peace to you who were far off and peace to those who were near. For through Him we both have access in one Spirit to the Father. So then you are no longer strangers and aliens, but you are fellow citizens with the saints and members of the household of God, built on the foundation of the apostles and prophets, Christ Jesus Himself being the cornerstone, in whom the whole structure, being joined together, grows into a holy temple in the Lord. In Him you also are being built together into a dwelling place for God by the Spirit. Ephesians 2:11–22

In these verses, Paul is speaking of reconciliation earned by the blood shed by Jesus Christ. The Jews lived within God's Old Testament covenant and under His Old Testament promise. The Gentiles, however, lived without hope. But Jesus' blood was of a new covenant. It reconciled Jews and Gentiles—all humanity became one in Christ's sacrifice (v. 14). Now everybody gets in on God's promise!

* * * * *

Jesus' blood created another incredible reconciliation: Jew and Gentile are now reconciled to God. The barrier of sin between God and humanity was insurmountable. Sin and eternal damnation created a chasm that no person could ever leap, a height we could never climb, a distance we could never run. But Jesus broke down that barrier. He filled that chasm. Now we can approach God by hanging on to Jesus. God hears us because of Jesus. God makes us His sons and daughters because of Jesus.

The battles we find ourselves fighting are of this world. Remember that the Big Fight has been fought and won for us already!

Conclude the session on a personal level—

6. A peaceful conscience

> But He was pierced for our transgressions; He was crushed for our iniquities; upon Him was the chastisement that brought us peace, and with His wounds we are healed. Isaiah 53:5

God knows that each of us struggles and each of us sins. Read Isaiah 53:5 aloud in first person, substituting "me" for "our" and "I" for "we." But He was pierced for *my* transgressions; He was crushed for *my* iniquities; upon Him was the chastisement that brought *me* peace, and with His wounds *I* am healed. Jesus shed His blood, and each and every person can rest in the comfortable warmth of a peaceful conscience. No amount of trouble in this world can take that peace away from us because Jesus defeated trouble once and for all. To reiterate God's truth: there is now a real peace between each believer's heart and God. What once was a great divide, caused by sin, between God and man has been spanned by Jesus' death and victory over sin.

Work in Progress: Taking It Home

As the study session concludes, review the six kinds of peace that were discussed. Can you come up with them without flipping back through the session pages? Take time to contemplate the following question:

Which one of these areas in your life today seems to be most lacking peace?

And the follow-up question, of course, is . . .

What can you do about it?

Be specific! By seeing the small bits, you will see that changing a situation is possible. It is easier to chew a small bite than a giant mouthful, after all!

* * * * *

As always, when the study group meets, talk bout these questions and answers together. Spend time listening, hearing, and encouraging.

Be sure to give time to anyone who has questions or comments before wrapping up. Close the session with a prayer. Begin with thanksgiving for the time spent in God's Word, then ask each willing participant to pray for or about each of the six types of peace that were discussed. The leader may close with a prayer of her own words, or your group can pray the following aloud:

Heavenly Peacemaker, we come to You today with thankfulness for the peace with which You grace us. We ask that our hearts always be open to feeling Your presence and Your peace. Grant our personal, local, national, and worldwide communities the desire to create peaceful relationships and the willingness to hear Your words, Almighty Counselor. It is in Jesus' name we pray. And all God's people say,

Amen!

Session E

A Work in Progress: Service

'Tis better to give than to receive

Introducing . . .

"Giving back" is popular these days: Joe makes a positive contribution to society, implying that he benefited from society at some point earlier in his life. Another hot term is "pay it forward." This concept is based on the "haves," who invest time, money, or both in the "have nots." The assumption is that the "have nots" will use the boost to become successful, then do the same thing—or "pay it forward" again—for the next group of up-and-comers.

What is the one-word description of both of these catch phrases? Service. Service with a smile. Customer service. We're here to serve you.

The expectation of service is as American as baseball and apple pie. The fact that there are hundreds of universities across the country offering degrees in hospitality tells it clearly. That expectation of service began way before America was even born. This study session looks all the way back to expectations of service in the Old Testament. We will begin with a closer look at the Law, which commands us not to be selfish, then tread into how we are to serve God and others. By now, you are sensing that the study will close on a high note. So as not to disappoint, the discussion will roll around to just how and why Christ serves us.

Get going!

Anyone work in hospitality?

As your group gathers, allow for a spoken response or show of hands from those who work in a service industry. Working together, make a list of what jobs are included in this employment category. Here's a start: waitress, bartender, cook, janitor, sales clerk, housekeeper, and driver . . .

Some United States service industry tidbits:

- An Internet search for "house cleaning services" yielded "About 117,000,000 results" (www.google.com, May 13, 2014).
- In 2013, the U.S. Bureau of Labor Statistics reported 12,353,300 employees in the Accommodation and Food Services sector (United States Department of Labor, Bureau of Labor Statistics, Occupational Employee Statistics, May 1, 2013. www.bls.gov).
- When a U.S. Department of Labor report includes sales clerks, cashiers, food prep and service, office clerks, customer service reps, and nurses, the U.S. service industry employment rate is one in every five Americans (U.S. Department of Labor, Occupational Employment and Wages Summary, April 27, 2014. www.bls.gov).
- McDonald's serves nearly 70 million people every day worldwide (www.McDonalds.com, May 1, 2014). The "service industry" can also claim professional services of accounting, architectural, engineering, legal, and management consultation. And we can include financial services such as banking, asset management, and insurance, plus all branches of medical services. The list goes on and on!

Who do we serve? Who do I serve?

This should be answered on a personal level by each individual. Keep in mind your own individual situations and involvements. When the group meets, compare your answers and lists.

Those are *our* thoughts. Now dig into God's Word to hear His thoughts on service.

1. Self serve?

Allow for volunteers in your group to take turns reading the following three passages aloud. Then talk about what they all may have in common.

> No one can serve two masters, for either he will hate the one and love the other, or he will be devoted to the one and despise the other. You cannot serve God and money. Matthew 6:24
>
> For although they knew God, they did not honor Him as God or give thanks to Him, but they became futile in their thinking, and their foolish hearts were darkened. Claiming to be wise, they became fools. . . . They exchanged the truth about God for a lie and worshiped and served the creature rather than the Creator, who is blessed forever! Romans 1:21–22, 25
>
> The story of Mary and Martha as found in Luke 10:38–42

Describe what it is to be selfish.

Then consider: Is it selfish to look out for number one? to focus on me, myself, and I? Is it the idea of prioritizing your needs and desires, then serving others with what is left? The world tries to convince us that there is no harm in the "me first" attitude. In the verses we just read, one could argue that the people are serving money, or created things, or the kitchen; they are not serving themselves. That, however, is the devil's advocate speaking. These folks are serving *their* chosen priority, focusing on what *they* can do. In essence, they are serving themselves. Selfishness is displayed when one places the highest priority on what he wants, needs, or believes.

The "serve God, not self" concept is tricky to grasp. There is not a concrete, black-and-white to-do list for Christians because we do, in fact, live in a world where we must take care of ourselves.

Take some time to probe the following question:

When does taking care of our needs turn into selfishness?

When your study group meets, share your answers with one another. There will be a variety of thoughts, and you will probably see that a gray area exists between "self care" and "selfishness." Whether or not a consensus is reached, the best advice comes from Jesus in Luke 10:42, where He says, "You are anxious and troubled about many things, but one thing is necessary." That one thing is belief in Jesus Christ. What flows from belief is a desire to do His will. Which leads us to . . .

2. Serve the Lord.

> Now therefore fear the Lord and serve Him in sincerity and in faithfulness. . . . Choose this day whom you will serve. Joshua 24:14–15

> Only fear the Lord and serve Him faithfully with all your heart. For consider what great things He has done for you. 1 Samuel 12:24

> Now therefore, O kings, be wise; be warned, O rulers of the earth. Serve the Lord with fear, and rejoice with trembling. Psalm 2:10–11

> It is the Lord your God you shall fear. Him you shall serve and by His name you shall swear. Deuteronomy 6:13

These four Scripture passages are not suggestions; they are commands. With your group, talk about the difference between a suggestion and a command. God does not politely say, "Hey there, Christian. Might be a good idea to respect the Lord. How do you feel about serving Him?" See, suggestions leave the door open a crack. God's commands close the door tightly: "Serve the Lord." Period. What other command is coupled with serving the Lord? Fear. We are to fear the Lord and serve Him. We unpacked the definition of fear in Session 2, when the focus was on respect. Fear is a reverential awe, a holding in the highest regard.

Is this type of fear only reserved for God?

Think for a minute: Is there any person for whom you have such respect for that the feeling crosses over into fear? Steve Jobs, Oprah Winfrey, Peyton Manning? Remember . . . reverential awe. This person does things with such amazing fluidity that you have a difficult time describing him or her. And if you had the opportunity to meet this person face-to-face . . . ? Perhaps you would stumble around on your words. Maybe you could come up with a bold handshake. Likely, you would have a willingness to do, talk about, or provide anything your guest desired. And there it is: fear and service dovetail.

> Then Jesus said to him, "Be gone, Satan! For it is written, "You shall worship the Lord your God and Him only shall you serve." Matthew 4:10

> How much more will the blood of Christ, who through the eternal Spirit offered Himself without blemish to God, purify our conscience from dead works to serve the living God. Hebrews 9:14

Okay, so we are to serve God. But as the opening of this session indicated, the act of serving involves doing something for another, may necessitate the use of hands, and implies another's dependence. But God does not depend on us for anything.

> Nor is [God] served by human hands, as though He needed anything, since He Himself gives to all mankind life and breath and everything. Acts 17:25

So, what does serving God look like?

> Serve the Lord with gladness! Come into His presence with singing! Psalm 100:2

Praising God is serving Him; showing Him the awe we have for Him is serving Him. That is Part 1 of what serving God looks like.

"Serve the LORD with gladness! Come into His presence with singing!"
—Psalm 100:2

Part 2 becomes clear in Matthew 25:31–45. Go ahead—read it all!

"And the King will answer them, 'Truly, I say to you, as you did it to one of the least of these My brothers, you did it to Me'" (Matthew 25:40). It is as simple as that. God cares *for* His creation *through* His creation. We serve God by serving our neighbor, which leads us to . . .

3. Serve others.

The desire to care for our neighbor is not solely a matter of Christian principle. It is a moral value that God instills in all humanity. Serving others is a popular philanthropic theme: the U.S. Postal Service's Stamp Out Hunger Food Drive, the Girl Scouts' April Showers Personal Care Items Drive, and Dr. Martin Luther King Day and September 11 are now thought of as National Days of Service in the United States. College admissions officers and scholarship administrators want to know areas and volume of applicants' community service. The corporate world encourages employees to serve in the community and often tracks volunteer hours.

Take a look at what God has to say in His Word; He is once again straightforward:

> Having gifts that differ according to the grace given to us, let us use them: if prophecy, in proportion to our faith; if service, in our serving; the one who teaches, in his teaching. Romans 12:6–7
>
> For you were called to freedom, brothers. Only do not use your freedom as an opportunity for the flesh, but through love serve one another. For the whole law is fulfilled in one word: "You shall love your neighbor as yourself." Galatians 5:13–14
>
> Rendering service with a good will as to the Lord and not to man. Ephesians 6:7

* * * * *

List some times and places in which community service is required.

answer on page 89

> "Rendering service with a good will as to the Lord and not to man."
> —Ephesians 6:7

Are you for or against the general policy of required service hours? List some positives and negatives associated with requiring people to volunteer their time.

Take time in your group study to share your thoughts and lists, especially, if some group members currently have or know someone who has "required service hours."

This brings up the question, Do you believe people have to be pushed to do the right thing? pushed to serve?

Sometimes, yes. It is not a human's natural inclination to want to serve, want to help, want to do for others. Why is this? Because we are often selfish and always sinful. And because we are sinful, we are in need of Jesus.

4. Christ serves us.

> For who is greater, one who reclines at table or one who serves? Is it not the one who reclines at table? But I am among you as the one who serves. Luke 22:27

Jesus first points out the conventional wisdom (which is still true today) that the one who sits at the table is greater than the one who serves. And then He makes His point: Jesus says He is the Messiah—the greatest—and He is not sitting! He is in the world to serve!

> John 13:3–17: Jesus washes His disciples' feet

> The Son of Man did not come to be served but to serve, and to give His life as a ransom for many. Matthew 20:28

Jesus, in His life, gave us the example of how to live, how to serve, and how to love one another. He humbled Himself. The King of kings did the dirty work. And in His death, Jesus not only *served* us but also *saved* us from spiritual death.

Work in Progress: Taking It Home

This week, end with some quiet time.

Identify two people to serve in the coming two weeks—two people whose paths do not normally cross yours.

Share your thoughts on this "Taking It Home" question with the group. Encourage one another, affirm intents, and feel a personal lift knowing that everyone in your group is going to stretch in the coming weeks.

Close with a group prayer, a volunteer's individual prayer, the leader's own words, or this prayer:

Dear Jesus, we thank You for the opportunity to gather today and hear what Your Word says to our hearts and for our lives. Strengthen our faith and our connection to You, that our actions rise as a response to the blessings You give us. Help us serve You out of the great fear and respect we have for You, and give us the grace to help others do the same. We praise You and thank You for serving us by giving Your life as our ransom. In Your name we pray. And all God's people say,

Amen!

Session F

A Work in Progress: Cooperation

Better to bend than break

Introducing . . .

Think back to elementary school, to the group project assignment—the one often met with a collective groan. Why was it sometimes difficult or even painful? The short answer is because of other people and their differing personal styles. Some of us are independent creatures, quick to form opinions and inclined to think (sometimes rightly) that our ideas are the best ideas. Others of us are completely comfortable following along, coasting in the draft of someone else's work. The subsequent melding of thoughts and styles can be as easy as peanut butter and jelly or as challenging as oil and water. Regardless, the fourth-grade group project was about cooperation, and it was just the beginning of a lifelong process of learning how to work together.

In this session, we will be reminded of several of God's cooperating teams. Our Creator put us all on this earth together and has a plan for us to overlap one another in work, in marriage, in family. When working together, different parts become a whole. The Lord asks us to cooperate, even expects it, for in cooperation, unity is built. Finally, we will see that although we often fail to cooperate, we have all been given a gift of unity. Galatians 3:28 sums it up: "You are all one in Christ Jesus."

Get going!

Name the speaker: "We have learned to fly the air like birds and swim the sea like fish, but we have not learned the simple art of living together as brothers."

answer on page 91

The speaker gave a lecture following his receipt of the Nobel Peace Prize. In it, he addressed the three issues he felt the world needed to be freed from: racial injustice, poverty, and war (Dr. Martin Luther King Jr., "The Quest for Peace and Justice," delivered Dec. 11, 1964; www.Nobelprize.org, May 2014). You may question why this quote was not part of the study session on peace. King was awarded the Peace Prize, after all. But consider this—to whom were King's words originally addressed? Not only blacks and whites, but also the "haves" and the "have nots," Catholics and Protestants. All people who were not cooperating!

Who could this quote be applied to today?

It could apply to some nationalities in the current global society, quite a few ethnic groups, all religious divisions, all political parties, all who are oppressed, and anyone who is on the high horse. In other words, people who are not cooperating!

* * * * *

King's comment is an echo of the American rallying cry "United we stand, divided we fall." The motto has been used throughout United States history and was born of the American Revolution. John Dickinson wrote "The Liberty Song" in 1768. Stanza 4 reads,

> Then join hand in hand, brave Americans all,
> By uniting we stand, by dividing we fall;
> In so righteous a cause let us hope to succeed,
> For heaven approves of each generous deed."
> (John Dickinson, "United We Stand," July, 1942. Smithsonian National Museum of American History; amhistory.si.edu, May 13, 2014)

"Living together as brothers" and "By uniting we stand." These writers, King and Dickinson, were separated by nearly two hundred years, but both had the wisdom to see the benefit of cooperation on a tremendous scale, and both saw its necessity.

* * * * *

Explain what it means to cooperate.

"The beginning of strife is like letting out water, so quit before the quarrel breaks out."
—Proverbs 17:14

answer on page 91

Cooperation comes in many shapes and sizes, from cooperating siblings to cooperating nations. But cooperation is always on display when two or more entities work together and encourage one another for mutual benefit. There are a couple of particularly important elements: (1) calm communication between two or more parties who think before acting or speaking, and (2) each party's willingness to listen to, consider, and act upon the proposals of the other party.

* * * * *

Now back to the Bible.

Teamwork as part of God's plan

God's Word presents examples of cooperating teammates. We can learn by observing:

Moses and Aaron

Beginning in Exodus 3, we read about God calling Moses to bring the Israelites out of Egypt. Moses was unmistakably dragging his feet; he did not feel qualified and had NO confidence in himself. The Lord countered, saying, "Oh, no . . . hold on. I will help you." Still Moses begged, "Please send someone else!" God met Moses halfway.

> Then the anger of the Lord was kindled against Moses and He said, "Is there not Aaron, your brother, the Levite? I know that he can speak well. Behold, he is coming out to meet you, and when he sees you, he will be glad in his heart. You shall speak to him and put the words in his mouth, and I will be with your mouth and with his mouth and will teach you both what to do. He shall speak for you to the people, and he shall be your mouth, and you shall be as God to him. Exodus 4:14–16

He proclaimed that Moses and his brother Aaron would be teammates. Moses and Aaron would cooperate, work together, and each use his strong suit to take care of God's work.

A group of four, including Joshua, Moses, Aaron, and Hur

Read about these guys, their teamwork and their cooperation in Exodus 17:8–13. God's plan of preserving the Israelites is accomplished.

A third team, Elijah and Elisha

We witness cooperation again, this time in 2 Kings 2:1–12. This mentor/apprentice relationship not only shows us cooperation, but also provides us with a great example of mutual respect.

New Testament Examples

> And He called the twelve and began to send them out two by two. . . . So they went out and proclaimed that people should repent. Mark 6:7, 12

In twos! Look at that! Jesus knows the value of cooperating teammates.

* * * * *

> After this the Lord appointed seventy-two others and sent them on ahead of Him, two by two, into every town and place where He Himself was about to go. Luke 10:1

In twos!

* * * * *

> Now there were in the church at Antioch prophets and teachers, Barnabas, Simeon who was called Niger, Lucius of Cyrene, Manaen a lifelong friend of Herod the tetrarch, and Saul. While they were worshiping the Lord and fasting, the Holy Spirit said, "Set apart for Me Barnabas and Saul for the work to which I have called them." Acts 13:1–2

Barnabas and Saul—two!

* * * * *

Barnabas and Mark, Paul and Silas

Read Acts 15:36–40. These verses begin with a breakdown of cooperation. Paul and Barnabas had an argument that ended with them parting ways. However, take note that, before their departures, they each found another teammate!

* * * * *

> Two are better than one, because they have a good reward for their toil. Ecclesiastes 4:9

God determined from the beginning that we humans would need each other. His Word gives us strong examples of this plan in action, and His words give us clear direction to implement His plan. Perhaps there is no better place to show this than through . . .

"There is neither Jew nor Greek, there is neither slave nor free, there is no male and female, for you are all one in Christ Jesus."
—Galatians 3:28

Cooperation in our marriages

> Then the LORD God said, "It is not good that the man should be alone; I will make him a helper fit for him." Genesis 2:18

What?! A helper? For who?! The implication here is that humanity was incomplete and in need of some additional traits. Adam did not have everything it takes—there just are not enough tools in one toolbox. A suitable helper was needed and was then created. Eve was given a different set of tools in her complementary toolbox. The differences between men's and women's natural inclinations and methods have been known to cause friction. These differences, though complementary, can be maddening. Such friction is not a part of God's design; it is the result of sin in our midst and hearts. God's plan is that life's work runs smoothly with two cooperating toolboxes—emphasis on cooperating!

God's words for the ladies:

> It is better to live in a corner of the housetop than in a house shared with a quarrelsome wife. Proverbs 21:9

> An excellent wife who can find? She is far more precious than jewels. The heart of her husband trusts in her, and he will have no lack of gain. She does him good, and not harm, all the days of her life. Proverbs 31:10–12

Now for some of God's straight shooting for the fellas:

> Likewise, husbands, live with your wives in an understanding way, showing honor to the woman. 1 Peter 3:7

> Husbands, love your wives, as Christ loved the church and gave Himself up for her. Ephesians 5:25

It works both ways, does it not? God desires cooperation: a joining of forces, encouragement of one another, and contribution for mutual benefit.

Where can cooperation spread beyond marriage?

Cooperation in our families

These next words, all from Proverbs, need no interpretation.

> The beginning of strife is like letting out water, so quit before the quarrel breaks out. Proverbs 17:14
>
> A brother offended is more unyielding than a strong city, and quarreling is like the bars of a castle. Proverbs 18:19
>
> A foolish son is ruin to his father, and a wife's quarreling is a continual dripping of rain. Proverbs 19:13

That is a double-whammy—one verse covering child *and* wife. Regarding the foolish son, all of us want our children to succeed in life. Because we love our children, we want the very best for them—at least what the very best is by our estimation. To be honest, though, part of the desire for our children's success stems from wanting our successful children to somehow prove we are good parents. And regarding the quarreling wife, remember the old saying about honey catching more flies than vinegar? No one responds well to a constant nag, nag, nag dripping in the ear. We *all* need to hear God's reminder to zip that lip sometimes, both as children and as spouses. Earlier, we used a metaphor about different tools in the toolbox. God presents a similar metaphor, and it may sound familiar. First, read the verses from Scripture as Paul wrote them for us.

> For just as the body is one and has many members, and all the members of the body, though many, are one body, so it is with Christ. For in one Spirit we were all baptized into one body—Jews or Greeks, slaves or free—and all were made to drink of one Spirit.
>
> For the body does not consist of one member but of many. If the foot should say, "Because I am not a hand, I do not belong to the body," that would not make it any less a part of the body. And if the ear should say, "Because I am not an eye, I do not belong to the body," that would not make it any less a part of the body. If the whole body were an eye, where would be the sense of hearing? If the whole body were an ear, where would be the sense of smell? But as it is, God arranged the members in the body, each one of

> them, as He chose. If all were a single member, where would the body be? As it is, there are many parts, yet one body.
>
> The eye cannot say to the hand, "I have no need of you," nor again the head to the feet, "I have no need of you." On the contrary, the parts of the body that seem to be weaker are indispensable, and on those parts of the body that we think less honorable we bestow the greater honor, and our unpresentable parts are treated with greater modesty, which our more presentable parts do not require. But God has so composed the body, giving greater honor to the part that lacked it, that there may be no division in the body, but that the members may have the same care for one another. If one member suffers, all suffer together; if one member is honored, all rejoice together.
>
> Now you are the body of Christ and individually members of it. 1 Corinthians 12:12–28

Now, read it again with the family in mind: the family is not made up of one member, but of many. What if the son were to say, "Because I am not a father, I do not belong to the family"? All body parts, from the brain to the baby toe, are designed by God to coordinate, cooperate, and function together smoothly. Likewise the give and take of family members contributes to the whole of family life. From cooperation within the small family unit grows the practice of cooperation within a large group and throughout life.

Unity: Cooperation in Life

> So we, though many, are one body in Christ, and individually members one of another. Romans 12:5

In this verse, the body metaphor pertains not to family, but to all believers in Christ. God desires (and expects) us *all* to cooperate, to work together amicably to do His will and do our work. Hear more cooperation appeals from God's Word.

> I appeal to you, brothers, by the name of our Lord Jesus Christ, that all of you agree, and that there be no divisions among you, but that you be united in the same mind and the same judgment. 1 Corinthians 1:10
>
> There is neither Jew nor Greek, there is neither slave nor free, there is no male and female, for you are all one in Christ Jesus. Galatians 3:28

> I therefore, a prisoner for the Lord, urge you to walk in a manner worthy of the calling to which you have been called, . . . eager to maintain the unity of the Spirit in the bond of peace. Ephesians 4:1, 3

These thoughts are becoming repetitious. Probably because God really means it!

> May the God of endurance and encouragement grant you to live in such harmony with one another, in accord with Christ Jesus. Romans 15:5

A spirit of unity—*that* is teamwork. We have all had the opportunity to feel the pleasurable, satisfying side of teamwork. We've been members of a family, choir, sports team, business partnership, production line, or clean-up crew. God wants us to know that spirit of unity, of togetherness, of a we're-all-in-this-together support system. And the warmest, most encompassing truth is that this unity God wants us to know is based upon *Him*. Our unity is founded on our trust in Him and is provided by Him. Unity in work and unity in heart—when God is involved in both places, we have nowhere to look but up!

Work in Progress: Taking It Home

Paul wrote many letters encouraging the faith of countless people. Many of this session's Scripture references were pleas of Paul encouraging the unity and cooperation of early Christians. His words are timeless, and they are meant for us as well.

Wrap up the session with two calls to action:

Encourage unity: With whom do you have a personal relationship that is a bit strained right now?

You may have to pick just one! Satan often gets us to focus on things that are wrong or "off" in a relationship. But God calls us to unity! Tell Satan to take a hike and write down a list of commonalities you share with that person. List similar interests, similar family situations, comparable job challenges, like personality traits, related goals. This week or month, focus on things that are *right* in that struggling relationship.

Encourage cooperation: Where would you like to see and feel a stronger "team" unity?

Brainstorm a short list of some possible actions you could take to help it happen. Circle your favorite two. This coming week or month, commit to actually *doing* them.

When your group meets for Bible study, share the thoughts you are comfortable sharing. Encourage one another, and even hold one another accountable for making positive change.

Close the session with an appeal for today's Christians. The leader may use her own words, or the group may pray the following together:

Dear heavenly Father, as our Creator, You know our hearts. You know that sometimes we each struggle to even tolerate our human companions, much less cooperate with them. Please forgive us for our impatience and for our selfish inclinations. As we heard in Your Word today, guide us to be helpmates to our loved ones and helpers to our worldly neighbors.

Thank You for the model of perfect cooperation among You, Your Son, and Your Spirit. Thank You for the victory over sin that made cooperation possible. Thank You for the grace You extend to us, which makes that victory ours. In Jesus' name we pray.

And all God's people say,

Amen!

Session G

A Work in Progress: Perseverance

Carry on!

Introducing . . .

Perseverance: that stick-to-it, keep-your-chin-up, try-and-try-again attitude that leaves little room for self-pity. America began through perseverance and was built on perseverance. Think of what the Pilgrims endured—the months-long voyage. In a cramped, musty boat. On the gigantic rolling ocean. Arriving to no shelter. In the winter. Who timed that trip?! No heat, no food. To say that they persevered seems an understatement! And think of the path to American independence—from those who dared to dream of it to those who convinced the masses it was plausible, to the vast numbers who dedicated themselves to pulling it off. This is perseverance as a broad concept, as a trait displayed collectively by a group, corporation, or even a nation.

Perseverance can also be thought of more intimately, on a personal level. "I endure hardship. I am not derailed by misfortune. I stick with it. I will succeed!" But sometimes, as the old saying goes, this is easier said than done. Life is hard! There are challenges we all face, hills we all approach, and curveballs we are all thrown. Life leaves us shouting, "Help, God!"

In this study session, we will again fill our thoughts with examples that God gives us in His Word. We will read of God's people who persevered. In challenging circumstances, God's faithfulness was there to carry and sustain. And we will see how this is true for us today too.

We often resign ourselves to struggling and straining through our daily lives and earthly situations. But what about our faith? Isn't having faith supposed to be easy? Isn't our faith supposed to be what *helps* us through struggles? The short answer, of course, is yes. But the reality of life on a sin-steeped planet is that even maintaining faith takes perseverance. Thanks, God, for not leaving us high and dry!

Get going!

The light man, the chicken man, and the mouse man: three creative minds; some might call them brilliant, some might say genius. Each man used his genius and creativity in very different ways. Think about what we would be without if these men had not persevered.

Among his many amazing accomplishments, Thomas Edison revolutionized the incandescent light bulb, vastly increasing its lifespan and creating a whole system of electric lighting. Edison must have known in his heart that his idea would work. His efforts failed more than 1,600 times before he perfected the glowing electric filament. His perseverance eventually helped light cities and boosted the spirits of night owls nationwide (The Lemelson Center for the Study of Invention and Innovation, Smithsonian Institution; http://invention.smithsonian.org, September 19, 2014).

Colonel Sanders perfected his recipe for "finger lickin' good" fried chicken. Sanders must have known in his heart that he had created a winning chicken experience. He began by cooking for patrons of his gas station and eventually sold his interest in KFC franchises for $2 million. Sanders's perseverance gave Americans nationwide an opportunity to line up and taste Kentucky Fried Chicken for themselves (http://colonelsanders.com/history, May 2014).

Walt Disney envisioned the magical empire of Disneyland. He must have known in his heart that his ideas would come together in greatness. His plea for financing his dream was rejected hundreds of times. Finally, Walt secured a deal to make Disneyland possible: an arrangement with executives at the ABC television network. Disney's perseverance began with the magical kingdom that has now taken on a life of its own (http://www.designingdisney.com, September 14, 2014).

With your group, recall the triumphs of Edison, Sanders, and Disney and mix in recollections of personal perseverance. Unfortunately, most people do not achieve worldwide notoriety, yet everyone perseveres and learns through trying experiences.

Drawing from your personal experiences and knowledge of others' experiences, list some elements of perseverance.

answer on page 92

During your group study, have each person tell which three they consider most important in defining perseverance. Consider things like hard work, persistence, and proceeding without complaint. Then check your answers against the suggestions on page 92.

This *is* a Bible study—now it is time to get into God's Word, beginning with some stories of folks who persevered.

Perseverance for lifetimes

Joseph, as told in Genesis 37–45

Individually, then with your group, summarize Joseph's tale of perseverance. As you read the chapters in Genesis, look for five big challenges that Joseph faced.

1.

2.

3.

4.

5.

answer on page 92

Joseph made the best of all situations he found himself in. He worked very hard, even as an outsider. And his faith allowed him to realize that, throughout his personal trials, God would show and share His faithfulness to His people.

> Do not be distressed or angry with yourselves because you sold me here, for God sent me before you to preserve life . . . to preserve for you a remnant on earth, and to keep alive for you many survivors. Genesis 45:5, 7

* * * * *

Moses, as told beginning in Exodus 3

Joseph's perseverance was through big stuff—slavery, imprisonment, isolation. Moses endured some different brands of perseverance. Again, summarize Moses' tale of perseverance on your own and then with your group.

Read Exodus 3–19 and look for seven frustrating events that might have made Moses want to beat his head on a wall.

1.

2.

3.

4.

5.

6.

7.

answer on page 92

Through two things, Moses' faithful perseverance and God's faithful forgiveness, Israel continued to be God's treasured possession and holy nation (19:5).

Joseph and Moses persevered throughout their life's work—work that was for the benefit of others. And God was faithful to them. Read these New Testament verses with Joseph or Moses in mind:

> Therefore, since we are surrounded by so great a cloud of witnesses, let us also lay aside every weight, and sin which clings so closely, and let us run with endurance the race that is set before us. Hebrews 12:1

For this is a gracious thing, when, mindful of God, one endures sorrows while suffering unjustly. 1 Peter 2:19

Blessed is the man who remains steadfast under trial, for when he has stood the test he will receive the crown of life, which God has promised to those who love Him. James 1:12

Our two guys, Joseph and Moses, fit right into these verses, don't they? In your group meeting, take time to read the verses aloud—or read them silently on your own—this time applying the words to yourself.

"For Your steadfast love is great to the heavens, Your faithfulness to the clouds."
—Psalm 57:10

* * * * *

Perseverance in personal events

Now, therefore, thus you shall say to My servant David, "Thus says the Lord of hosts, I took you from the pasture, from following the sheep, that you should be prince over My people Israel." 2 Samuel 7:8

This verse makes it sound so simple and easy: God named David king. Easy as that. Kings can do whatever they want! No need for a king to have perseverance, right? But consider the words of King David:

My soul is in the midst of lions; I lie down amid fiery beasts—the children of man, whose teeth are spears and arrows, whose tongues are sharp swords. Psalm 57:4

For behold, they lie in wait for my life; fierce men stir up strife against me. Psalm 59:3

Hear my voice, O God, in my complaint; preserve my life from dread of the enemy. Psalm 64:1

Look to the right and see: there is none who takes notice of me; no refuge remains to me; no one cares for my soul. Psalm 142:4

In real life, the man was a great and powerful king. He led many troops and fought many battles. He worked hard and found success. Yet these verses are clear—he worried and struggled through many real fears and dangers. He was a real guy with a common psyche. And he persevered. God was faithful to him.

For Your steadfast love is great to the heavens, Your faithfulness to the clouds. Psalm 57:10

> I give thanks to You, O LORD my God, with my whole heart, and I will glorify Your name forever. For great is Your steadfast love toward me; You have delivered my soul from the depths of Sheol. Psalm 86:12–13

* * * * *

Now we will hear another familiar story: the birth of John the Baptist. Perseverance is not the usual focus, but today we will search for it.

Read Luke 1:5–25, 57–66. Find three examples of perseverance in the story.

(Although thoughts on the answer are included in the Session Notes, this may be a good question to work at on your own, without looking at the Notes. At your small group study, share the answers aloud. Maybe there is more perseverance in here than you think!)

1.

2.

3.

answer on page 93

What God has to say about perseverance

> It is for discipline that you have to endure. God is treating you as sons. For what son is there whom his father does not discipline? Hebrews 12:7

> My son, do not despise the LORD's discipline or be weary of His reproof, for the LORD reproves him whom He loves, as a father the son in whom he delights. Proverbs 3:11–12

* * * * *

A final biblical example of perseverance, probably the one you have been expecting all along:

> Now there was a day when the sons of God came to present themselves before the LORD, and Satan also came among them.

> The LORD said to Satan, "From where have you come?" Satan answered the LORD and said, "From going to and fro on the earth, and from walking up and down on it." And the LORD said to Satan, "Have you considered My servant Job, that there is none like him on the earth, a blameless and upright man, who fears God and turns away from evil?" Then Satan answered the LORD and said, "Does Job fear God for no reason? Have You not put a hedge around him and his house and all that he has, on every side? You have blessed the work of his hands, and his possessions have increased in the land. But stretch out Your hand and touch all that he has, and he will curse You to Your face." And the LORD said to Satan, "Behold, all that he has is in your hand. Only against him do not stretch out your hand." So Satan went out from the presence of the LORD. Job 1:6–12

That is the beginning of the story. Then Satan proceeded to take all of Job's livestock and children. Job's reaction:

> And [Job] said, "Naked I came from my mother's womb, and naked shall I return. The LORD gave, and the LORD has taken away; blessed be the name of the LORD." In all this Job did not sin or charge God with wrong. Job 1:21–22

Job is still smiling, somehow. But then:

> Satan went out from the presence of the LORD and struck Job with loathsome sores from the sole of his foot to the crown of his head. Job 2:7

Job's reaction to his bodily afflictions:

> His wife said to him, "Do you still hold fast your integrity? Curse God and die." But he said to her, "You speak as one of the foolish women would speak. Shall we receive good from God, and shall we not receive evil?" In all this Job did not sin with his lips. Job 2:9–10

But the suffering gets old, and Job's smile fades. He questions why he is still alive, and he questions God's plan. Yet Job perseveres all the way through chapter 37. Then the Lord speaks to him through a storm.

> And the LORD said to Job: "Shall a faultfinder contend with the Almighty? He who argues with God, let him answer it." Then Job answered the LORD and said: "Behold, I am of small account; what shall I answer You? I lay my hand on my mouth." Job 40:1–4

> I know that You can do all things, and that no purpose of Yours can be thwarted. I had heard of You by the hearing of the ear, but now my eye sees You; therefore I despise myself, and repent in dust and ashes. Job 42:2, 5–6

Job came to realize that his perseverance was a means to an end: he came to know, understand, and trust God more fully through his trials. Surely we can learn from Job's experience and also learn the same lessons through our own trials. Part of persevering is acknowledging our mistakes and moving forward on a better path. Read what God has to say about that:

> Behold, we consider those blessed who remained steadfast. You have heard of the steadfastness of Job, and you have seen the purpose of the Lord, how the Lord is compassionate and merciful. James 5:11

> And we rejoice in hope of the glory of God. Not only that, but we rejoice in our sufferings, knowing that suffering produces endurance, and endurance produces character, and character produces hope. Romans 5:2–4

> No temptation has overtaken you that is not common to man. God is faithful, and He will not let you be tempted beyond your ability, but with the temptation He will also provide the way of escape, that you may be able to endure it. 1 Corinthians 10:13

Note that the Greek for "tempt" can also be translated as "test." Using that translation, the tests we endure are common tests. Talk with other members of your group about where these temptations and tests originate. From God? No, these negatives in our paths originate from sin—sinful flesh, sinful Satan, sinful world. But God knows that, and still uses "all things for the good of those who love Him" (Romans 8:28). God knows that people think and learn when they are forced to persevere. Maybe this is the discipline spoken of in Hebrews 12:7: "It is for discipline that you have to endure."

* * * * *

Perseverance in our faith

Part of being able to persevere is knowing that God is full of compassion and mercy. Part of perseverance is having faith in God's faithfulness. And part of perseverance is knowing that we may never see the end of temptations or troubles in this life, but that, through Jesus, God promises us resolution in heaven.

Let us not grow weary of doing good, for in due season we will reap, if we do not give up. Galatians 6:9

Therefore, my beloved brothers, be steadfast, immovable, always abounding in the work of the Lord, knowing that in the Lord your labor is not in vain. 1 Corinthians 15:58

But as for you, continue in what you have learned and have firmly believed, knowing from whom you learned it and how from childhood you have been acquainted with the sacred writings, which are able to make you wise for salvation through faith in Christ Jesus. 2 Timothy 3:14–15

I am coming soon. Hold fast what you have, so that no one may seize your crown. Revelation 3:11

"Let us not grow weary of doing good, for in due season we will reap, if we do not give up." —Galatians 6:9

What parts of the previous four verses are most meaningful to you?

Share your favorite phrases or your favorite verse among the members during your group Bible study.

Remember that, yes, the faith of everyone does falter sometimes. Our desire to persevere in life and in faith does slip. But God's Word is for us. It encourages us with its truth and God's promise carries us forward: heaven is ours! Salvation belongs to the believer!

Work in Progress: Taking It Home

This session's biblical stories of perseverance focused on Joseph, Moses, Elizabeth, Zechariah, David, and Job. Those poor people! Think of a struggle or two that you are currently enduring that is similar to something one of those six fought through. Write your thoughts here. Then, if you are willing, share your thoughts with your group.

Who are you feeling most like these days—Joseph, Moses, Elizabeth, Zechariah, David, or Job?

Joseph: Lost? Separated or unconnected from loved ones?

Moses: Unqualified? Weighed down by heavy expectations?

Elizabeth: Resigned? Maybe even embarrassed?

Zechariah: Skeptical? Just going through the motions?

David: Constantly fighting fires? Bearing up under attack?

Job: Victimized? Helpless and out of control?

One great thing that God's Word does is provide real stories of real people who went through real hard times. By knowing these stories, today's Christians can feel encouraged, knowing that God cared for His creation then and He will care for His creation today.

As we reach the conclusion of *A Work in Progress,* reflect on your personal accomplishments through the study and share them with your group.

This has been a journey of becoming a better person—more responsible, respectful, compassionate, peaceful, devoted servants of our neighbors. And why are we on this journey, anyway? Hopefully, through the past sessions, all will have been reminded that we strive for betterment because we are compelled to honor God who gave us life and serve Him in appreciation of His majesty. "You're awesome, God! I'm going to give you my best!"

We leave this session on perseverance and this series on personal progress by revisiting 1 Corinthians 10:13:

> No temptation has overtaken you except what is common to mankind. And God is faithful; He will not let you be tempted beyond what you can bear. But when you are tempted, He will also provide a way out so that you can endure it.

Clearly, each of us is tempted by our selfish humanity *all the time.* Although we want to do right, although we strive for personal betterment, we cannot keep God's Laws. Yet the Gospel rings true! The *best* thing God's

Word does is explain how Jesus has paid the price for our sins. We are forgiven. God *has* provided a way out for us, a way to endure. He is Jesus.

Allow a member of the group to close with prayer, or have some time for all to pray silently. Close by reading the following prayer aloud:

Dear Father, we know that You manage all that happens here on earth, in our communities, and in each of our homes. Today, we thank You for our blessings and praise You for being the one that governs it all.

Please be in our hearts as we run the races You have marked out for us. Give us some grit to stand up, and give us perseverance to hold fast to our faith in Jesus as our Savior. Help our minds to be open and ready to learn from the environments and situations You lead us to. And keep our eyes always on the end goal, which is eternal life with You.

Thank You for the great blessings of friendship and shared journeys. It is in Your Son's name we pray. And all God's people say,

Amen!

Session Notes

Session A—Responsibility

We are responsible for guarding our own faith and the faith of others as well.

Community: Rights and freedoms.

Faith: Our faith and the faith of others. We guard your own belief in Jesus and witness it to others.

Personal: I am the only person who decides what type of person I am.

Session B—Respect

Just what does it mean to be respectful?

- Respect is showing regard and appreciation based on the other person's position.
- Respect is holding someone in high esteem.
- Respect is giving weight to someone's thoughts or intellect.
- Respect can be shown as politeness, bravery, restraint, or a willingness to speak up.
- Respect can look like breaking out of your comfort zone or keeping well within the boundaries of your position.
- Respect is often demanded, but it is worth far more when given freely.

Unscramble answers: **Feelings, Opinions, Rights,** *and* **Values.**

Session C—Compassion

The six generations living in America today include:

- The G.I. Generation, or the Greatest Generation, born 1901–1926
- The Silent Generation, born 1927–1945
- Baby Boomers, born 1946–1964
- Generation X, born 1965–1980
- Generation Y, or Millennials, born 1981–2000
- Generation Z, or the iGen, born 2001–

(www.genimperative.com, retrieved November 21, 2014)

What does it mean to be compassionate?

Compassion is "sympathetic consciousness of others' distress together with a desire to alleviate it" (*Merriam-Webster's Collegiate Dictionary*). It is demonstrated by service and generosity. It is a desire to ease suffering.

Why do you think Jesus healed people?

Some were healed to provide a witness to Jesus' power as God the Son, as proof of His divine nature. Some were healed in response to the faith of the afflicted. Many were healed simply as the result of Jesus' compassion.

Describe the lawyer. Why did he want to "justify himself"?

The lawyer began with a most serious question: what he must do to be given eternal life. And, being a thorough man, his follow-up question was for clarification. He really wanted to know if he was doing it right. He wanted to obey the law, and in order to do that, he had to know who to love, whom he should treat as he himself wanted to be treated.

How might we explain the lack of compassion from the religious professionals?

Maybe they were in a hurry, on their way to a synagogue where many were expecting them. Or maybe they didn't want to dirty themselves by helping a guy who was a mess. Or maybe they just didn't care.

Session D—Peace

Frank's mantra was "Serenity now." The ironic part was that he often shouted it with uncorked fury, "SERENITY NOW!"

***Brainstorm some terms, phrases, and slang that use the word* peace.**

–peace of mind

–not a moment's peace

–Peace Corps

–peace on earth

–peace talks

–peace sign (two fingers held in a *V*)

–*War and Peace*

–make peace

–"peace be with you"

–peace treaty

–keep the peace

–disturbing the peace

–Prince of Peace

–world peace

–justice of the peace

–"Peace out!"

Peace is the presence of tranquility, quiet, harmony, and order and the absence of worry, conflict, strife, turmoil, tension, anger, and hatred.

Session E—Service

List some times and places in which community service is required.

Here are a few to get the group started:

1. High schools. A certain number of documented community service hours are required for graduation.
2. Congregations. Members are "expected" to fill various volunteer spots.
3. Elementary schools. Parents are required to serve a number of hours through the school year or pay a buyout fee to be excused from volunteering.
4. The United States penal system. Community service hours are routinely required as punishment or retribution for offenses committed.
5. The United States government. Citizens are required to serve on jury duty. (Not quite volunteering, but almost!)

Discuss the reasons behind the "for it" or "against it" points of view.

The positives behind requiring service hours are that it

- can increase awareness of the needs of the community and prompts individuals' realizations that they can fill some of those needs;
- plants seeds for future service;
- presents an opportunity for teaching God's single command to love our neighbor; and
- serves the community and takes care of people.

The negatives of requiring service hours are that

- service under these terms is not a byproduct of faith;
- service under these terms is not necessarily a byproduct of good will; and
- service is done because of man's rules rather than because of God's command.
- if community service was not required by worldly organizations and institutions, the community at large may be served less.

Session F—Cooperation

Name the speaker: "We have learned to fly the air like birds and swim the sea like fish, but we have not learned the simple art of living together as brothers."

These words were spoken by Dr. Martin Luther King Jr. on December 11, 1964.

Cooperate: Co = with, or jointly; operate = perform, or work.

Session G—Perseverance

List some of the elements of perseverance.

For example: hard work, persistence, proceeding without complaining . . . keep going!

Five big challenges that Joseph faced:

1. Sold into slavery by his brothers (37:28)
2. Worked for Pharaoh's captain (39:1)
3. Imprisoned for over two years (39:20)
4. Worked for Pharaoh for nine years, storing up grain to feed Egypt during the seven-year famine that he dreamed about (41:36–57)
5. Didn't see his father or brothers this entire time

Seven frustrating events for Moses:

1. Installed as leader of the Israelites against his will; "Please send someone else!" (Exodus 4:13).

2, Talked things over with Pharaoh, who, in response, greatly increased the Israelites' workload; the Israelites' response? "We hate Moses" (5:21).

3. Told the Israelites about God's promise to free them from Egypt; nobody listened (6:9).

4. Plagued Egypt through God's commands; when one was not effective, he tried another—ten times (7:14–11:10).
5. Having left Egypt, the Israelites were now *so hungry*. And grouchy. And telling Moses all about how they wished they were still in Egypt (16:3). Can you hear Moses shouting, "Are you people kidding me?!"
6. The Israelites were thirsty and surly to the point that Moses asked God, "What am I to do with these people? They are almost ready to stone me" (17:4).
7. The Israelites promised to obey God and keep the covenant (19:8), then snubbed God and built a golden calf to worship (32:7–8).

Examples of Zechariah and Elizabeth's perseverance:

1. Persevering through disgrace. The life situation by itself called for some perseverance. Zechariah and Elizabeth had prayed for a child (v. 13) and they had been praying for a long time (v. 18). A childless couple was "disgraced" among the people (v. 25), and Zechariah and Elizabeth had to live with that.
2. Persevering in prayer. Zechariah and Elizabeth were childless and old. They had been praying for a LONG time.
3. Persevering through hardship. An angel visited Zechariah and announced the upcoming birth. Zechariah—who was, by this time, and old man—questioned the validity of that statement. As a result, he got to persevere through nine months of not being able to speak. (Probably best NOT to question an angel of the Lord.)